This...
...is about life.

Book II: Fulfill Your Dreams

a collection of poems from 1974-1995

by Randi Owens

This...

...is about life.

Book II: Fulfill Your Dreams

a collection of poems from 1974-1995

by Randi Owens

By: Randi Owens

Editor: Emily Autenrieth

Illustrations: Kimberly Gallardo

Contributors:

Carlos Owens Jr

Copyright ©
Printed in the U.S.A.
ISBN 978-0-9981443-1-3

First Edition 2016

For each of you,
dare to dream...

Table of contents

An Introduction: First Years in Brief

1974

    On My Way to College 2
    How Fire Begins 3
    My Friend Gwen 4
    I Give Up 5
    What Is The Meaning Of Hate? 6
    Why Dream? 7
    The Death Plot 8
    A Lying Friend Is Not True 9
    The Ocean So Blue 10
    Window Washers 11
    My Life of Dreams 12
    A Short Stop for Me 13
    They Are Human, Too 14
    Adam 15
    Mary 16
    The Tiny Hill 17
    If I Don't Pass 18
    That Feeling of Sorrow 19
    High Hopes 20
    Happy Birthday to You 21

1975

    I Stand Alone at the Doors 24
    Our Arrival 25
    Young Love... and I Still Love You 26
    Do We Deserve Better? 27
    You're Always By My Side 28

Table of contents

1975
- The Circle that Thought It Was a Square 29
- The Impossible Dream 30
- Inspiration 31
- My Truth of Love 32
- Why Me? 33
- The Shaky Thief 34
- I Want to Be Rich 35
- Some People and Their Thoughts 36
- Maria Q. 37
- Green 38
- Basic Training...Sgt. Kitto 39
- Ask Yourself...TSgt. Williams 40
- Flight 109...Basic Training 41
- Trust 42
- Elena, I Remember 43
- Capricorn Eli 44
- Crying 45
- A Small Romance 46
- As I Watched My Window Darken 47
- I Was Meant to Stand Alone 48
- From Iris to Ireland 49
- Money Hungry Witch 50
- True Lovers 51

1976
- The Night Lover 54
- What if This Was the End 55
- Daddy, Please Don't Cry 56
- Feelings 57
- What is Your Objective 58

Table of contents

1976
- Pedro, Don't Go 59
- C. M. Puckleberry 60
- The Image of Me Today 61
- My Momma 62

1977
- Our First Wedding Anniversary 64
- There is Lasting Pain and Forgiveness 65
- On This Day 66
- Our Love 67
- You Are Going to Make it 68
- Only God is a Real Friend to Me 69
- My Friend Hui Chiu 70

1978
- That Hurting Feeling 72
- What Was Taken... Is Forever Lost 73
- Leaving Me Hurt and at a Loss 74
- No Christmas 75
- Smiles and Cheers 76
- Only Once 77
- To Be Known 78
- Zarranda Zoe 79
- From Beginning to End... Starting All Over Again 80
- Pain 81

1979
- Failure 84
- Little Kenny Knottingburg: How Old Are You? 85
- Looking Within to Decide 86

Table of contents

1979
- Why Doesn't Somebody Give? 87
- My Nobility at Risk 88
- My Wish, Dream, and Prayer 89
- You... Yourself! 90
- It's Strange 91
- Out in the Country 92
- Sonny and the Yankees 93
- How Can I Help You...Lost in Between 94
- Happy Valentine's Day My Love 95
- Morie 96
- Do You Love Me 97
- If I had Two Days to Live, I would... 98

1980
- Fraternal Twins 100
- Missing you 101
- With You Gone 102
- Miss Fat Pat 103
- The Democracy of Today 104
- Did You Know...? 105
- Decisions 106

1982
- The Battle of Regret 108
- The Death of a Poem 109
- A Lack of Faith 110
- Let This Be a Special Day 111
- Traveling Home 112

Table of contents

1983
- Lost Art 114
- Don't Look at Me 115
- My Symptoms of Pain 116

1984
- I have Found What I Was After 118
- Easter FUN 119

1987
- You Remind Me Of... 122
- Look at The People 123
- Spiritual Food Cake 124

1989
- Graduation 126

1990
- The Flower of my Dreams 128
- If You Want to be Truly Happy 129

1992
- Silly Sandy 132
- Transition 133

1995
- I Feel so Dead Inside... 136
- You and Me 138
- A Mother's Suffering...Don't Give Up 139
- I Carry My Cross...Memories 140
- Friendship 141

Introduction

I wrote the following poems over a period of 21 years, beginning when I was focused on venturing into life as an adult and continuing forward into the birth of my four children. They proved to be a valuable lifeline when I believed I was alone and needed to forge my path in life if I were to succeed.

Poetry can provide therapeutic relief from worries and life's excess stressors. It invites readers to incorporate their thoughts and emotions into the words, creating the opportunity for temporary breaks from everyday life encounters. Through the poems, I learned that it was ok to be upset, smile, laugh and cry ... and to simply live. We can intertwine and cross what's real with what's fantasy ... if only just for that moment in time. I invite you to enter into the world of a young woman willing to dream of possibilities in life, bringing to light your personal thoughts and emotions along with you.

1974

On My Way to College

I may not make it to college on just my concentration
It's better to be on my way regardless of the situation

Sitting around doing nothing is not what I have in mind
Getting out to show my gratitude for what I've been through is more in line

I know college costs a lot of money, maybe even more
But it's better to get an education than to sit around and become a bore

On my way to college, to me, is a most important dream
I'll never make it until someday I choose to fulfill that dream, it seems

How Fire Begins

Fire in the woods moving towards mother nature to destroy with its flames
Has a life of its own as it stretches out while avoiding the slight rain

The people watching the fire believe that with the little rain it will be doused
There are others running home to find a way to protect their house

How fire begins is with a cigarette, camp fire, lightning, or accident
The crackling sound of the heat as it burns everything in its path without relent

There is goodness to fire if started in the right way
It provides for cooking, bathing, and warmth in a place to stay

I fear fire if it gets out of hand and has no control
How fire begins is with respect for the living thing it is as it unfolds

My Friend Gwen

I often wondered what it would be like to have a friend so true
It never crossed my mind to think that friend would be you

You are very social and popular, and I don't know why
... You'd choose to be my special friend and walk at my side

You'll not remember what this is all about, I'm sure
It meant a lot to me because it was so honest and pure

You have a beautiful laugh that draws others into your fold
You are always inclusive with your smile and your friendship role

Gwen, I want to thank you for your kindness, sincerity and all
For being my only friend and listening without judging me for my faults

I Give Up

Nothing seems to be on my side
Most things I do wrong, which hurts my pride

If I feel down I try to smile anyway
Yet somehow my feelings show on my face

Maybe someday I'll simply give up, and not let it bother me so
But will that day ever come? Today, I just don't know

What Is the Meaning of Hate?

I cry because I know who hates me
And I wonder why they won't let me be

Though I am down on my knowledge of how to hope
I feel I may have to find a way in life to cope

The deep meaning of hate I cannot fully describe
There are times when it hurts so bad until I just want to die

I understand the value of life and that there is much the future will be revealing
Hate, like love, is a strong emotion and if not tempered, the pain is a physical feeling

Hate is never the answer and seldom about you
When we truly love ourselves, it is difficult to hate someone else too

Why Dream?

Why should I dream, I've been told twice
I don't have a chance of going to college at today's price

I wasn't dreaming when it was told to me
I was excited at the possibility

Why should I dream when it may be true
I may as well give up and keep serving food

I want to do more with my life and my dreams take me there
Why dream when others tell me I'll go nowhere

My dreams give me focus and a reminder to stay strong
I can't stop dreaming and I plan to prove them wrong

The Death Plot

In every ditch on every side
There's a body near the street that no one tried to hide

The death plot was bad and fear did abound
It was really sad to see so many bodies on the ground

Old women, children, and babies alike were ordered to be killed
The media sought the stories and were not always sensitive to what was real

When war prevails, there is little sorrow or pity for the dead's plight
Their actions were fueled by words of "hate, kill, and destroy" as they began to fight

No one was safe from the death plot as the orders were fulfilled
Don't leave anyone alive, they said … they all have to be killed

The innocent along with the guilty had fled
The soldiers had no time for discretion as they were shot at and bled

Burn the village, destroy the fields
Move out and find those running for the hills

Dry your eyes, soldier, there is no room for tears
Follow orders or prepare to be court martialed and imprisoned for years

No one is perfect and there is no single faction to point at and say they did wrong
There are many to share in the guilt of the murders of the innocent that are gone

So many innocent were caught up in the massive war that came
Many that participated had to live with the devastation, and later, the shame

A Lying Friend Is Not True

Once I thought I had a true friend
But this thought soon came to a sad end

I could not trust her with my greatest fears, be they near or far
Because she would lie about everything in order to feel like a star

She could not stop when she began with the attention garnered for her behavior
She'd stretch the truth and tell a lie with no remorse as she sought everyone's favor

There was a time when she was but a shadow, believing she was never good
    enough to be first
I befriended her, encouraged her, and sought to draw forth her inner self worth

Do not lie, but tell the truth, it is that which will help you to feel free
Learn of honesty and to yourself be true as you grow to accept who you can be

The Ocean Water So Blue

When the surf is high and the tides are low
The teams all rush to be the first to go

If the water is up and the oceans wide
You'd better run if you want to catch the high tide

Riding on the ocean waves for some is new,
But it doesn't take long until they know what to do

The ocean water is not as cool as the great sea floor
It's a long way from the center if you don't use a sturdy board

As you lie on your board to begin to paddle out
You look back as your friends support you with a shout

Slowly, you seek to balance your body as you begin to stand
Courage is a reminder that the board and waves are yours to command

The oceans water is blue, the day full of sunshine
You smile as you ride the greatest wave of your lifetime

Window Washers

Window washers seem to be mostly men working, sometimes up very high
They look happy as they clean the windows so close to the sky

I think a window washer should be a woman, old and mean
So that when she stops washing the windows they will really gleam

I forgot how brave some men are and how afraid some women may be
Being so far above ground could limit how far anyone would want to see

I guess window washing is not so great until you learn how
A woman can learn as well as a man with the technology available now

My Life of Dreams

I've dreamed of becoming someone that can make a difference and have power
I cannot say which of my dreams will influence me more in my greatest hour

I've often dreamed of becoming a musician, a drummer in a band
I've dreamed of making a difference in any way I can

Have you ever had a dream like that,
where you play a drum, flute, violin, or clarinet?

Many girls talk of dreams of boys that are tall and handsome, seldom short or stout
While boys often talk of dreams of cars that mean more than the girls they take out

I often dream of writing and taking the opportunity to use my voice
In my dreams I'm in the background because no one wants me as their first choice

In my life dreams, I break through the barriers and speak of the good I perceive
I allow my brain the freedom to formulate and express what I someday hope to achieve

Perhaps a teacher has had dreams of learning to teach
Maybe their life dream was to somehow educate every child within reach

There is so much more to my life dreams, but here I will stop
As I ponder the life dreams of others who no longer appreciate what they've got

A Short Stop for Me

I know I need to rest, and so I'll stop right here
I hope I won't fall behind because to me, this is a great fear

Though you may not know it, a poet needs a short stop once in awhile
It helps to improve their ability, which they've had since being a child

I've written a few poems, and have plenty more to write
Without my innate ability, I wouldn't have them in sight

Back to work with me, I can't rest on just this one poem, you know
I have much work to do, so on with it I must go

They Are Human, Too

Have you ever seen the children, the ones who live alone
Have you ever seen the children, the ones without a home

Have you ever seen the old lady, her beauty and glamour gone
Have you ever seen the old lady, she lives for another day's dawn

Have you ever seen the little girl, roaming the streets for food
Have you ever seen the little girl, never in a happy mood

Have you ever seen the baby, the one paralyzed for life from abuse
Have you ever seen the baby, the one to whom touch and love are refused

Have you ever seen the wonders of nature, the ones prepared with delight
Have you ever seen the wonders of nature, the ones that don't seem right

Have you ever begun to think of how strange life seems to be
Have you ever stopped to think that they are human like you and me

Adam

He is a once-in-a-lifetime guy that's too easily upset
The girl that wins his heart hasn't learned very much yet

Adam is okay, I guess ... at least he's pretty cool
He's pretty smart about some things, but with others, he's kind of a fool

He talks of the facts of life as though he knows them all
He sometimes makes you angry enough to beat your head on a wall

Adam is what would be determined as big-hearted and fair
Although at times he's outspoken, leaving his heart open and bare

There is knowledge in life that you must learn to accept as fact
As there is much knowledge of things in life I know that I lack

Adam means little or no harm in the words that he speaks
He doesn't sort through his words first to ensure the correctness of those which he seeks

No, no one's perfect ... we all harbor a fault or two
Adam is no exception in a life fraught with so many things to do

Adam lives in a world surrounded by his dreams
He thinks of himself, mainly, as strange as it seems

There are books that speak of love, of how it is today
Adam's book of love is as it will always stay

So, he is no exception with his good deeds, as well as his faults in a life of potential insanity
No, no one is perfect, I'm sure it wasn't meant to be, as Adam adheres to his own
    understanding of humanity

Mary

Mary, with all of my heart, these words I say
My thoughts of you grow stronger each day

I hope that soon, we'll be together at last
To talk of our future as we set aside the past

Mary, my love for you is quite true and full of heart
Though my words are few, they are but a mere start

As time goes by and the days become few
I am constantly dreaming of the moments I'll spend with you

You're kind, sweet, and my dream come true
Mary, I am trying to say "I love you"

Let not the wind, breeze, or cold air so free
Keep my sweet Mary away from me

The Tiny Hill

The tiny hill was standing tall
... Or thought it was, but it was really held up by a wall

The tiny hill was not really a hill at all
... just a small sand pile standing near a hall

The tiny hill was very small in height
... you could see over it if you had very good sight

One day the poor tiny hill was quite overrun
... now it is flat as the ground and was swept out into the sun

If I Don't Pass

If I don't pass my exams ... which I sure hope I will
It'll be pretty bad for me out in a world so real

I really struggled and studied hard to pass all of my tests
I feel that with my English class I may not have done my best

I know it's difficult to study for so much at once ... but I try
I work hard to succeed by doing more than just enough to get by

My teachers are very calm with the things they say for the exam prep
I listen attentively, taking notes and comparing the past weeks tests step-by-step

If only I could do better with my grammar, I'd feel relief about the rest
I want to think in my mind that I knew the answers and had no need to guess

Well here goes, tomorrow is do or die day and I am an emotional wreck
Tonight, I'll study a little longer and hope it's enough to pass once everything is checked

That Feeling of Sorrow

I'll never forget that look of sadness on the face of Ken
The way he stood and watched me as if I'd committed a sin
He frowned as I walked away from my once very good friend

Somehow we'd made it work even though we were of a different race
We didn't live too far apart, went to the same school, and shared the same space
One day the friendship vanished when he turned to see the look on my face

The shock of the conversation once overheard
... was followed by a broken friendship without a word
Before that we had something in common as two nerds

I miss my friend and the way we'd both smile
At the reactions of others as we walked pass with our books in a pile
I miss how we'd drink Kool-aid and talk after walking for miles

That feeling of sorrow goes both ways with the loss
The race doesn't matter as long as true friendship remains at all costs
I regret that neither of us understood what we'd so carelessly tossed

High Hopes

If you want to fly you've got to have hope
Just like to take a good bath, first you need soap

To be hopeful is up to you in your own way
Without hope you'd be as good as dead every day

It takes hope not to just give up and cry
It takes hope not to wish you could die

If you want to forget hope because you fear getting old
There's still some left with years to go on your soul

Happy Birthday to You

Today is someone's birthday, someone we all know
I plan to wrap a present, topped with a great grand bow

"Happy Birthday to you," I would say
I wish you happiness all through your day

The name of the person I am speaking of
Is someone I am sure that we all love

I hope they don't feel the need to be shy about their coming age
Instead, consider it another number to add to their wisdom phrase

A Birthday Celebration is an opportunity to share yet one more year
We get another chance to start over as we make our coming wishes clear

1975

I Stand Alone at the Doors

I'm standing alone at the doors of a stranger,
wondering should I go in and accept my fate or should I linger

I'm about to leave when the doors began to part,
I turn around to look up and stare with a start

Within those doors reside my judges of confession,
and there is no way for me to run away from their ordained profession

The statement is now being passed around into all of their hands,
until it finally reaches the one with the greatest authority to command

I kneel down to hear the conviction to which I am innocent of the crime,
when the verdict, "not guilty," is spoken loudly, I am grateful not to serve time

Mercy was taken upon me and I no longer stand at the doors feeling forlorn
My fear is for others, should this trend of malice continue, with concern
    for those yet born

Our Arrival

Our arrival at Lackland AFB was greeted with glee
a smile on the TI's face and a frown we could not see

It is now 0500, all airmen will be out of bed
down to the chow hall for your faces to be fed

Your first introduction to your team members and team chief
their words are so shocking until they leave you in a state of disbelief

Your training has started from that day on
you're free to learn, but not free to roam

After a while of marching and drilling each day
Your TI's first words of confidence are, "What can I say?

"… You march like babies, you drill like fools
… And I don't think you will ever improve"

You try and you try so hard to do right
Yet your TI continues to bark you into a fright

One day your TI walks in smiling and talking as if you are all his daughters
That smile leaves & the talk halts as he says…"how long can you tread water?"

Young Love ... and I Still Love You

Without your shining eyes aglow
my heart would fail to pound, you know

It is for you I live day by day
with your words of love that in God's name I pray

Should I bargain and lose your heart
I feel I would surely fall apart

It is your walk, your talk, and your love
which makes me give thanks for you to God above

Throughout the hardships, the sadness, and all of the pain
I still get chills when I hear your name

I hope and I pray that when it's all through
I can continue to say, "and I still love you"

Do We Deserve Better?

I felt lost and had been wronged, but you were gentle, understanding, & made it all right
We were married and for a while content, but then came the fights

Do we deserve better? I don't know
What I feel for you, I try to show

The respect you so willingly gave with warmth and open arms
Has changed to anger, profanity, frowns, and a feeling that I could be harmed

Do we deserve better? I am hopeful as I pray
I still remember the beautiful individual with whom I fell madly in love on that day

I believe life to be short in the scheme of things to come along
My lessons learned were harsh, but because of what went wrong, now I am strong

As I turned and looked back down the roads I've traveled, there were many falls & pain
I am grateful I survived my past and that I can move forward because of my life gains

Do we deserve better? Only we can truly say
Are we happy as we are, or do we go our separate ways?

I so desperately wanted "Happily Ever After" I didn't read the fine print, though bold
Is what I left behind still with me? is this what I have to look forward to as I grow old?

What do we want--not you, not me, but "We"?
For in truth, it is "We" that will succeed and "We" that can be free

Do we deserve better? Perhaps you are what's best for me and I have made my choice
Like a lifeline in the middle of the ocean, I can sink silently below the surface or I can
    grab on and have a voice.

You're Always by My Side

I walk the streets while I'm all alone and sad
I'm thinking of you and the love we could have had

You're always by my side no matter where I am
I seem to see you near me even when I'm in a jam

If you were ever missing from your space within my heart
I'd cry until you returned and all over we would start

Maybe I don't know what love really means
but when I'm with you it's not as bad as it seems

You are tall and handsome with a calm demeanor like mine
… but you're a guy and can replace me by your side at any time

The Circle that Thought It Was Square

The circle that thought it was square often remained behind
It thought it would slowly mature over time

One day the circle rolled down a hill
Landing in shavings of wood chips near a saw mill

The circle was now broken and feeling lost with shame
It knew it needed to heal while rolling away from blame

The circle viewed it's surroundings with relief knowing it wasn't square
It wanted to be accepted by others and not be in despair

The circle was put in a place of prominence where it could oversee all
It appeared pleased with it's location on the old log cabin wall

The Impossible Dream

To dream of being a high priest living above all
… may indeed be a dream of fantasy from which you are bound to fall

To reach your climax in life when you are about to give in
… is the chance you've taken often, once you decided to win

To dream of returning to your youthful days of childhood
… is a dream passing through your maturing mind to be understood

To dream of the ancient periods now long departed
… is to think on the times in history that we've pledged to keep guarded

To sit and stare into outer space with nothing apparently on your mind
… is to daydream of impossible things to do, and you never seem to have time

To look at your textbook in class and speak out loud
… is to wake from a dream and give the wrong answer with a shout

To dream of walking with your head high as you reach each life goal in stride
… is to carry yourself with dignity and grace, accepting compliments with pride

Inspiration

Inspiration is a common factor that can cause you to do more than you think
Once you feel inspired, a light goes on causing the mind, body, and spirit to link

There are those that are inspired to do their very best
There are those that are content with doing entirely less

There are those impressed with thoughts, which to them are well said
There are those that have few wise thoughts to consider in their head

There are those inspired by an opinion but they hold back for fear of disgrace
There are those offering inspiration for knowledge that should not go to waste

There are those reaching heights they never thought possible
There are those accepting success where before they only struggled

There are presenting opportunities to inspire others to voice thoughts over time
It only takes one to open the door of inspiration, making sure no one feels left behind

My Truth of Love

Although our love has been deep and true
I hope it will stay this way between me and you

My truth of love keeps me happy, not sad
but tell me my heart, why you act so bad

If our love is to be this way
we must have nothing else to say

If we get married and live all right
I don't want you to have another girl in your sights

Your temper you cannot control, although I wish you would
because if we get married, I want you to act like a good husband should

Now that I have shown my truth of love as you can see
I wish you would show yours by saying there's no one else but me

I'll keep this as my token of love which grows like a seed
In the hope that someday it will show through all of your growing needs

Why Me?

There are some things in life that are only dreams
As my love for Carl was, it seems

Sure, I've lost a few heart battles before
Should this heart I win, I would battle no more

I walked the road, searching in the rain
overlooking my hurt, ignoring my pain

I often think and wonder why
… should it be me to always cry?

Pity and sympathy for me I have none
for my brain is the key which ignites my heart to love only one

My world, my beliefs, my thoughts of how things should be
there remains always a questionable door without a key

I looked forward to his voice, his words, and his touch
for to know Carl was near to me meant so much

When the events of the past cross my thoughts, I see
… that same, repeatable question so strong: "Why me?"

The Shaky Thief

The shaky thief was not all that bad
He stole many things that he never had

Although this thief hated to take the things that were not his to steal
He could not stop because of how it made him feel

The shaky thief was very nervous and couldn't control his emotions
He had to have the things he took for his own personal devotions

One day he decided to suddenly stop as he realized that stealing was wrong
The shaky thief was no more as he worked hard to return things he'd brought home

I Want to Be Rich

I want to be rich and do things my way
... to have enough money to buy anything I can say

If I were rich I'd build many stores
... only to tear them down and build many more

My money won't last me for all time
If I were rich I'd waste it all at the drop of a dime

Some People and Their Thoughts

If everyone would try to understand
No one would make outrageous demands

We sometimes do what we have to do
And yet, there are many who do what they want to

There are those who think of the feelings of others
There are those that forget we are all sisters and brothers

People are like things--they too can fall apart
They may look bad but still be good at heart

Some people look happy every once in awhile
Then there are those people that very seldom smile

Some people really care about the things they may say
The world will be a better place to live if we all care more in some way

Maria Q.

Stand up and fight for your body rights
If Pedro isn't the answer, you're free to reassess your plight

When you were considering a relationship that binds
You had to think through your concerns as you hoped all would be fine

You said you'd decline and moved away to take a seat
While there you received an opportunity to prevail over a possible defeat

When it was time for your brain to engage, you were at your best
You knew you were at the top with your advanced intellect

You weren't happy with how you looked but you said it would do
You made a few adjustments and accepted what you had too

You decided to stand up for your body rights
You believed that you were worthy of your personal fight

Your body is your temple, a precious commodity
You are beautiful and Pedro says he's in love with all that he can see

Green

Height is not bad on a girl--at 6' 3"
Green was taller than the average girl, you see

She has wings on her feet and feathers in her hair
She has trouble with her dates ... she has to kiss them on a chair

She has a smile that truly shines
She has a walk that's smooth as time

She is tall and she is lean
She is as elegant as a queen

Her arms are long as they dangle at her side
She holds her head high with a great sense of pride

Green leads a life that is difficult and hard with little money or clout
She's a pleasant young lady and others want to be in her space when she's about

Basic Training ... Sgt. Kitto

She was our guide when we thought we couldn't go on
She brought out our military bearing when we thought to give up and go home

She would say we were looking good when we felt like we looked lost
She held us together when we couldn't seem to get across

She taught us to drill while standing right by our side
She brought out our wholesomeness while making us feel pride

There were mornings she would come into the barracks with a frown on her face
There were more mornings when she smiled and everything just fell into place

We learned to appreciate her understanding, her kindness, and her care
But most of all, we wish to thank her just for always being there

Ask Yourself, TSgt. Williams ...

How long can you tread water?
As long as we can make it to our destiny bound
How long can you tread water?
As long as we can swim and not drown

How long can you tread water?
Until we pass the requirements of basic training
How long can you tread water?
Until we find out what is the meaning

How long can you tread water?
Until we get it together, I'd say
How long can you tread water?
It depends on our TI from day to day

How long can you tread water?
Until the smile is wiped from your face
How long can you tread water?
Until you leave Lackland Air Force Base

How long can you tread water?
Ask yourself as you march about
How long can you tread water?
Until your training is complete and of your skills you have no doubt

Flight 109 - Basic Training

March on, Flight 109 … we can bear the heat and stay in line
March on, Flight 109 … we know that our steps are keeping time

We've looked over Lackland and what did we see
A band of TIs coming to set us free

March on, Flight 109 … the sun is bright but we're doing fine
March on, Flight 109 … remain in formation and don't fall behind

We hold our heads high as the heat beats down
March on, Flight 109 … if we lock our knees, the TIs will frown

March on, Flight 109 … together we are keeping in step
March on, Flight 109 … if one falls down, we can't stop to help

Get it together one more time … always unified Flight 109
We pivot to the left, we pivot to the right, always we step in time

We follow the lead and march on with the flight
We trust in each other to keep the line straight and formation tight

March on Flight 109 … six weeks have ended with orders set aside
March on Flight 109 … we await our assigned base with dignity and pride

Trust

God placed his trust in me
It is through his eyes that I see

It is his wisdom, his knowledge, his love and concern
… Providing me with a few of his traits I have learned

I thank him every night as I praise him every day
God is the light that guides me on my way

He is with me when I need him, he's always at my side
My trust in him grows stronger as each day I take my life in stride

Elena, I Remember

Some friends are just a case of smiling faces
They wish they had your life or could trade you places

You are somewhat different in that you show your concern
Through you I'm beginning to trust as your lessons I learn

You seem to give from the deepest depths within your heart
As I watch and listen, I recall feeling lighter in spirit from the very start

Your generosity is appreciated and well accepted too
I would like to tell you "thanks" just for being you

I know you have many troubles and pains of your own
When others come to you troubled, you simply leave your troubles alone

You bring a smile to even the saddest face in the room
You remind us that when there is triumph, we can't think of doom

I remember the many laughs and smiles that you brought about
I remember the small frowns when you couldn't figure things out

I remember your look when you felt as though the world was on your shoulder
As I look back, I remember you wished you could start your life all over

We often talked about the world being much larger and the people a little colder
When I look upon your face, I remember that you are much wiser and much older

I want you to remember that when you need a friend or life becomes a bore
Know that you can call or come to me because my heart to you is an open door

Here's wishing to you all of the very best
Elena, I feel that you deserve no less

Capricorn Eli

Some people say they can look at the world and know of its doom
Eli often looks past the stars and never sees the moon

A smile on his face you will seldom see
As if, within him, joy is not meant to be

He seems unusual in many things he may say or do
In that they take the fun from life as well as from you

He is not entirely a Mr. Scrooge--there are times when he'll smile
So seldom are those times that you may visualize them only for a brief while

There is potential for joy and goodness in everyone, and Eli is no exception
He has done many good deeds, some without noted perfection

Crying

I cried at a funeral and I cried as I traveled across the sea
I've got to quit crying, no one is crying over me

When I cried at the funeral it was sorrow and grief
As I cried while traveling over the sea, it was a great relief

Because there was happiness on the ship as we crossed
---giving me time to briefly forget about my loss

When crying at the funeral, it broke my heart in two
While crying on the ship, I thought of starting my life anew

Crying in the shower in the dead of night
---helped to heal my torn heart with memories of my plight

I find that I shed fewer tears as the years go by
I am creating my own happiness with little need to cry

A Small Romance

There is more to love than just the looks
There is more to romance than what's in the books

You can take a chance
--and develop a small romance

I've heard you say you don't quite understand
Why it is so difficult to hold on to your man

Woman, you've been trying to do that man harm
Ever since he came home late, setting off your alarms

You were stingy with your love and held back with your kiss
Seldom do you offer your heart enough for him to have anything to miss

When you got married it was "until death do us part"
But each time you have a conversation, the arguing starts

What kind of love are you showing each other with your choice?
You should be making love instead of in anger raise your voice

Have you each forgotten about your love and sexual healing demands?
Take time away from everyday life to have a little romance

As I Watched My Window Darken

In my heart, I have a strong memory of when my window grew dark
There was little light beyond the candle providing a small spark

Every night as I lay in bed, I'd think of the life that has gone away
I'd think of how I'll be alone again in a room that smells of decay

Up in the sky with all of the stars gone from the mist of night
I watch as a flicker of sunlight grows, smiling at such as beautiful sight

Night has fallen once again and I am alone as before
I watch my window darken as I listen to the local folklore

The people are moving about but no one speaks to me
As I watch my window darken, I am the ghost no one can see

I Was Meant to Stand Alone

By the way I am pushed around and hurt at heart so often in spite
of the kindness I show others, I feel that it just doesn't seem right

I try to treat everyone fairly as I hope they'll treat me the same, but instead
I was meant to be alone with thoughts of putting a bullet in my head

I overheard that people dislike me because I talk funny and I'm ugly
The ones I thought were friends laughed the loudest at what was said about me

I was meant to stand alone with no one to come to my rescue
I have had to stand strong when I didn't know what else to do

I was meant to stand alone with no time for pity or sorrow
I want to live today ... but I'm not sure about tomorrow

From Iris to Ireland

Iris was from England, a beggar from the streets
One day she begged for money and received a slab of meat

She loved to cook, and so she shared her seasoned meal
Everyone talked about the beautiful girl and her tasty veal

She went to Ireland which was her destiny
… vowing she'd return someday to see dad, mom, and me

She cooked a meal for the king who had a handsome son
Iris was poor no more when he sought her heart and won

The young Prince of Ireland had fallen in love with her
His father was disappointed and wanted him to marry another

The prince thought about his wishes, saying "Iris is the only one I'd consider
Although she has no money, she is worthy, and I love having her near"

Iris asked her family to move from England to Ireland to complete her joy
She sometimes cooks for her love in the kitchen where she was briefly employed

Money Hungry Witch

There was once a woman and money hungry was she
Her old mother died and left no money to pay the burial fees

The money hungry woman turned into a witch
She considered burying her mother in the backyard in a ditch

Once she allowed her anger to cool
She realized she was acting like a fool

The money hungry witch thought about the kindness her mother had shown
Realizing she'd been blessed with a car, no bills, and a debt-free home

When reality settled in, so did the shame of her mother's only child
As the money hungry witch used her money to bury her mother in style

She learned lessons about life and money and how easily they can disappear or perish
She realized that what her loving mother left behind were precious memories to cherish

True Lovers

If a boy says he loves you, don't take his word on that
He said the same thing to several other girls first ... the dirty rat

Tell him you don't care whether he's in love with you alone
Then remind him of the weekend he was late coming home

Tell him you're no fool and the relationship is done
Because you know he cannot prove you're the only one

Feel happy with your decision and the things you have said
And don't regret sending him off to a less informed girl's bed

True love goes both ways when the heart is involved
If he doesn't really love you the sadness will eventually dissolve

1976

The Night Lover

I met my lover on a train one night and we didn't talk much
We just enjoyed being close enough to each other to touch

On the night of our wedding day we had a celebration
We went to bed "to rest," he said … "I have to do a lot of concentration"

I thought my lover loved me but this wasn't a fact
He had another love and wanted to get her back

If you ever have a true night lover, listen to what is said
His promises to love and honor may not be the only crap you're fed

The night lover sought solace in my loving embrace
His lust for me and love of her made me rethink my attraction to his face

What if This Was the End?

Some people say that the end is pretty near
What if we are close to the end? Does it matter what we hear?

If we were bad and put in jail
We'd think it was the end if we had no bail

To be thrown into prison would be about the same
If this was the end, would we feel shame?

If this was the end, what would we have to fear?
We've all had our chances since we've been here

What if this was the end--should we run and hide?
Or, perhaps, take inventory of what we are like on the inside

Daddy, Please Don't Cry

Daddy, please don't cry, we'll be alright
Although God has called her away, he has foresight

At mother's funeral it was difficult for you to pray
As you began to cry over the casket where she lay

The loss was great, you didn't expect her to die so soon
... leaving you with six babies on Monday just before noon

We know you had to work and couldn't always be there
... placing us with people you trusted, hoping for their gentle care

We came home from school one day and were told that you were gone
I remember feeling sad, but mostly, I felt all alone

Memories of your gentleness gave me strength from day to day
I tell stories to your grandchildren of how much you both wanted to stay

Feelings

Feelings are strange and many are true
So are my feelings for you

To me you're more than just a shoulder to cry on
It is you who removes the hurt and pain of my being alone

I'll try hard ... and harder each and every day
To accept your friendship, which before me you so innocently lay

As others laugh behind my back I know I'll not be able to look you in the face
Because in my heart and mind, my feelings have gone astray

Your walk, your talk, your every smile, even your eyes that shine
---bring out the joys which are in my so often closed mind

What I feel and wish to say would take 10 pages or more
Should you read this carefully, you'll find that 10 would've been an unnecessary bore

Feelings are beautiful, though they can cause pain
I pray this poem you'll understand because there are many things it does explain

What Is Your Objective?

What do you think this is, a world bid by your rule?
Did you really believe them when they said, "Use your mind, it's your only tool?"

What manner of being do you think I am?
Should I wait while you act, as though you don't give a damn?

What in the world makes you want to plead your case?
What makes you think I'll allow you to take my God's place?

What is your objective, and why continue to plead
for a place of honor in my life when there is no need?

How dare you bring about your thoughts so cold?
… I care little for such news as yet unforetold

What is your objective, which makes you be so selfish and act carelessly?
How can you praise your failings and treat the success of others so unfairly?

Pedro, Don't Go

Leaving me just can't be
... what you're telling me, baby

Our love is young and yet so strong
I'm sure there is more right than wrong

Your short notice of departure really brought me pain
Should I ever lose your love, I would surely go insane

When I'm with you, I'm content in your arms
I can only think of your heartbeat, so tender and warm

The grass grows tall and green as does my love for you
I believe my love and affection will never cease but instead remain true

I belong to you
--for as long as you want me to

My heart and love for you are here for the giving
Because without you, life is not worth living

When you stand and stare at me from afar
the moon seems to encircle you wherever you are

The stars above have a beautiful shine
As my love for you has throughout time

Pedro, no words can express the way I feel
As no amount of money could pay our love expense bill

C. M. Puckleberry

C.M. Puckleberry was happy with a simple life
She didn't want very much, except to be a good wife

C.M. was tall and skinny, or rather slender and toned
She liked going to the gym but was tired of going alone

C.M. was very quiet and seldom made a fuss
She moved at a gracious pace because she didn't like to rush

C.M. Puckleberry cooked healthy meals for her friends
She enjoyed entertaining those in support of her trends

C.M. Puckleberry has worked at the same place since getting her college degree
She is fine smiling and getting paid for something she'd willingly do for free

C.M. Puckleberry was happy when she met her future groom and mate
He enjoyed many of the same things as she and fell in love on their second date

C.M. felt complete and happy with her new love and plans
She had patiently waited for her perfect wedding and for the right man

My Image of Me Today

I can't move like the others can
They have rhythm when they dance

I don't have a voice that draws others into my song
That requires a gift appreciated when coming from your lungs

I can't play an instrument with any true conviction
But I respect those who do so without any restrictions

The source of my image as it stands today in kind
Is based only on my ability to write and to share my mind

I choose the image of me that I wish to display
Because only I can decide on what others may think of me someday

My life isn't perfect, and I will leave no one in awe
There will be only me to blame should my image be flawed

My Momma

Long after you were gone, if I needed love or warmth you were always there
In your special way, I knew that it was your presence enfolding me with care

When I needed you to tend my wounds and hurts
You were there in my heart with silent words of comfort

Momma when I was down and feeling sad
Seeing your smile in my head made me glad

When I'm troubled you're the first memory to come to my aid
This is one of the many reasons my love for you will never fade

Sometimes, Momma, I feel like hiding behind a door
But when I think of what you would say, I feel like hiding no more

It would always be you to bring out my best
It was you who would set my mind at ease and at rest

Momma, because of you, I have answers to many of my prayers and desires
It is when I recall your welcome advice that I know I will never tire

It is with this in mind
--I pray that in time

Should my children ever need me
--no matter where I am, available to them I will always be

It is not everyday that one would be so blessed as to say
Even in death, you are there for me as through God I pray

I Miss You, Momma!!

1977

Our First Wedding Anniversary

One year today we are together,
Hoping within our hearts it is forever

You're my life, my love, my everything
When I look into your eyes, my heart still sings

Our unborn child, a token of our love
God, though unseen, watches over us from above

When, each night, I kneel down to pray
I thank God for you in every way

We've seen a great deal in our short period of time
Our coincidental meeting, an even stranger coming together of minds

Here's to gratitude and thanks on our very first wedding anniversary
With many more to come in the future years filled with love and harmony

There is Lasting Pain and Forgiveness

I feel nothing, as if I am surrounded by a fog in the dark of night
I have no will to confront the pain and no strength to fight

Seeing them together had created an emotional stain
I'd cried my tear ducts dry as I absorbed the lasting pain

I was past my delivery date and the doctors said, "you're overdue"
I felt as if I watched my life shatter through dreams where I had no clue

I'd often walk a distance in the hope of helping with the birth
Knowing in my heart he'd be born soon, as my belly was at the limit of its girth

Five days since walking in on them unexpectedly and my mind struggled to believe
But the instant replay was there throughout the baby's delivery

While in my fog of deception, I heard my son scream to life as if through stormy gusts
Still, I felt little as the love of my life had all but destroyed my trust

It was as if someone had taken a chunk of my heart from my chest
I'd always felt unworthy and his actions solidified my thoughts of being less

I held on because of the precious life God had given into my care
I was determined to pull through and provide our son the love I had to share

I offered him the opportunity to leave and go on his way
He said that he loved me and if I'd have him, he wanted to stay

Forgiveness is never easy but it's worth consideration
To judge another does not guarantee your salvation

I will always bear the scar where my heart was torn apart
With the birth of my son, my life did not end--instead, it created a new start

I chose to confront and address my pain through conversation and tears
Once my questions were answered, I chose not to bring it up again during future years

On This Day

The wait was long and the contractions a pain
He was overdue, but he finally came

What a precious gift I have to behold
My baby boy was born with all of his fingers and toes

He doesn't cry a lot, mostly when he is hungry or wet
He is a little watcher of the doctors and nurses we met

We named him a Jr., as was always our plan
He is such a beautiful baby that God has placed in our hands

He weighed in at 8.4 pounds and 22 inches long
He had a kick with a punch on legs not yet strong

As I held him in my arms close to my heart of memories on this day
I will forever remember my sweet baby as in my arms he lay

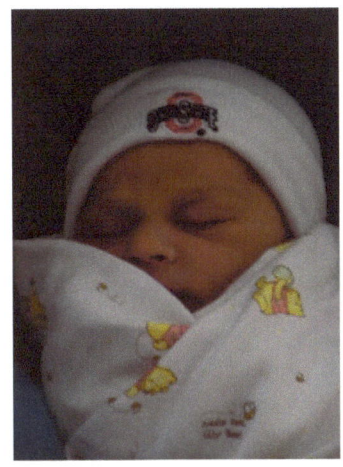

Our Love

I can remember a time when I could say our love was for real
Now I find it difficult to say these words as though I love you still

Do you remember the last time we were together?
Your words to me were, "Let's stay in love forever"

Well, my love, you have that look in your eyes once again
It is the look that tells me you are my only man

Now I feel confused and certain that I don't understand
Is it the look of love, or is it time for me to make other plans?

I've thought your last words through
And there is only one thing left for me to do

I've decided to set my heart free
And hope that someday you'll return it to me

You Are Going to Make It

You've climbed many passageways and walked many hills
For all of your suffering, what have you yet to give?

You are going to make it, although your aims in life are far
Someday you will have those things; your man, house, children and car

Sure, you will lose some things along the way
… but that is life … what else can I say?

You will win more because of your determination
You have a strong sense of self and will take more out of life before its deterioration

Thanks to the many changes brought about in strife
You will lead a rather glorious and interesting life

Don't give up or falter when you're near to the ending
Your future looks better than ever, considering what it was in the beginning

You are going to make it, this my life I'll wager
The minor things are not for you, your life is strictly for the major

Congratulations, may I be the first to say
I told you that you would make it, and here you are today

Only God Is a Real Friend to Me

You're alone ... but you are not
You're at the bottom ... but you're on top

You're happy and together, although sometimes sad
You see that what you have now is more than you once had

Your husband, children, and home are for you well deserved
You achieved where you are through both courage and hard work

Your prayers are being answered, although you believe slowly in turn
It took time to acknowledge wisdom as it will take time to retain what you learn

You're young and ambitious with a solid mind
You have a full life to carry forward and a lot of pain to leave behind

You have forgiven with love while you walk in pride
You believe you will succeed with God at your side

You hesitate to accept your intelligence and charm
You're growing to accept that you can recall the painful past with little or no alarm

You know now what you did not know then
You have learned to trust that God is more than your friend

My Friend Hui Chiu

Hui Chiu is a friend of mine whom I love and respect very much
Once our family moved away, we gradually lost touch

We have much in common because she is from my generation
There is a cultural divide due to our opposing lives and education

Although our families were together for a very short time
I've not forgotten her kindness and her bright smile of sunshine

My friend is dear to me and the positive things about her remain true
She'd often remind me to be happy and enjoy the things in life that I do

1978

That Hurting Feeling

First you take my heart in the palm of your hand and you squeeze it tight
Then you take my love and pretend it's not there as you spend time away all night

You take my pride and you throw it up against the wall
Then you take me in your arms and in love with you again I fall

Sometimes I think I'm dreaming the things I see when I'm awake during the day
Then I look back over my memories and I know I'll be lost forever if I stay

I realize that my feelings for you are not all gone
Then I also know that the things you do to me are wrong

Why can't you see that my life with you is filled with gloom?
But then you don't know that every day I come home, I sit and cry in our room

The things that you are doing to me are really hurting my mind
But then I feel that you will never change, and so we won't start over this time

What Was Taken ... Is Forever Lost

Hold tightly to the corners where the shadows are when the lights go on and you're in place
What was taken is forever lost, yet you hold on when you're found by God's good grace

When you have one hand in the dark and a foothold in the cold
Keep holding tightly to the crack that leaks out your soul

One foot in the gutter and the other on the sand
Hold onto the sun with a steady hand

As you reach and grab onto what's familiar and grip something real
You still hold onto tangible sorrows without having to really feel

I'm sorry I couldn't be more
... Sorry I didn't relax to see deeper into the core

I couldn't really see past myself to agree
It was selfish, I know ... and perhaps stupid of me

But it is what it is and I am who I am, no more and no less
It was devastating to endure ... leaving me with the weight of it on my chest

What was taken is forever lost
Leaving me to live with the burden of the cost

Leaving Me Hurt and at a Loss

With him, within the warmth of a cocoon, I am without
His cruelty shatters me and I want to shout

Do you still love me … No I dare say not
Do you still want me … No but I'm all you've got

Are you happy that we ever met … No I think as the tears flow
You leave me hurt and at a loss with the pain I keep deep lest it show

The line that divides in bed divides in home
It keeps us apart and each of us alone

Love is strength that binds us together
As we reach for each other, we can only get better

Sarcasm hurts as it intends
Leaving me in shreds, with little hope to mend

Humiliation finds joy in proving me wrong while giving my heartstrings a steady tug
Often I feel like a vessel for sex without caring preparation or gentle love

No Christmas

There is no Christmas to beat my Christmas to you
On this Christmas day, I hope you feel the same way too

As our ages gradually increase over the years
I'll think of your gift to me with loving tears

The gifts of a lifetime are the best to give
They never break but remain as long as we live

I am grateful for your gift and I won't turn it down
The one you searched for so long and finally found

There is no Christmas I would wish for more
Than the one where we are together, rich or poor

Merry Christmas to you, and your gift is under the tree
The coming years will be happy as we let our love flow freely

Smiles and Cheers

Smiles and cheers to all that I know
My love to them I will forever show

The smiles I give are to all I see
They may mean little to them, but a lot to me

My cheers I will greet each and every friend
I appreciate their patience and love for me within

When I put them together, they are my heart
Proving to me that my smiles and cheers are doing their part

Only Once

Only once did I have to look at the world of evil and hate
 ... in order that I might see and someday recall that it is never too late

Only once did I have to look at several faces in the crowd
 ... in order that I might see and someday recall their silence as others spoke aloud

Only once did I have to cheat on a test in a class
 ... in order to have learned that I need not have cheated to have passed

Only once was I invited to be a true lady in grace
 ... in order to see my dream come true of being dressed up in lace

Only once was it necessary in order that I might understand
 ... that you treat others the way you want to be treated as much as you can

Only once did I challenge to look at the world through God's eyes so clear
 ... as I reach towards those on the outside equally as I do those I hold most dear

To Be Known

I wonder how it would feel to be known
… to live a life all on your own

… to have servants wait upon you
… to have the world appreciate all that you do

… to have knocks at your door almost every hour
… to have the entire world under your power

… to live in a mansion in "Poverty Hills"
… to be someone known for your many skills

I wonder how it would feel to be known
… to live a life all on your own

Zarranda Zoe

Zarranda Zoe had the eyes of a lantern that glowed at night
She never tried to do anything unless she was sure she could do it right

Zarranda Zoe had teeth that were as white as ivory
She had a heart that was big and open and free

Zarranda Zoe had hair that was long and black as coal
She had a personality that made others want to be part of its golden glow

Zarranda Zoe was a child that cared for the world itself
She was the kind of person that didn't want her pains felt

Zarranda Zoe would often sit and stare out into a world far away
She had a mind that was wise as she showed kindness every day

Zarranda Zoe would sometimes ponder life far beyond her reach
She wanted to please those that were worthy and, to others, kindness teach

Zarranda Zoe was one in a million, with feelings she shared with others
As she lay on her bed paralyzed by her disease, she remained hopeful
… that we could learn to love one another

From Beginning to End ... Starting All Over Again

The trees are uprooted, they're dying away fast
The wind is still blowing; how long will they last?

You look out your window and what do you see
... your favorite vine is being crushed by a tree

From beginning to end, your work has been destroyed
You feel frustrated, upset, and a little annoyed

You sit down and begin to cry
... but soon you get up and dry your eyes

Your work of much patience, your torment and your toil
... are all being torn down and ripped away along with your fertilized soil

In the beginning you thought only of yourself and with great concern
Now the time has come to assess what lessons you have learned

Should the world be at its ending and the beginning lost in the past
You start a new world with new beginnings as you plant roots that will last

Pain

Pain for sale when it used to be free
A penny for your pains and troubled miseries

There are people in the world that are hurting inside out
There are those committing suicide thinking it will ease what the pain is about

Life isn't easy and for some it is pretty tough
They awake to find pain and any relief is never enough

Pain for sale when it used to be free
A nickel for your pains and troubled miseries

1979

Failure

Never say you've failed until you've tried it over and over again
It was not failure that brought about so many successful plans

Had Philo Farnsworth stopped at his first failure with the invention of the TV
Where would all of America's couch potatoes be?

You can say "I've failed," but is it really true?
Was your failure a false step or one brought on by you?

We fail at some of our greatest attempts in life, trying as hard as we can
Does this mean we should just give up and never try again?

"Failure, why, I've never seen the likes"
It is not failure which allows the underdog to win the fight

What was that word once again?
So your memory has "failed" you and you don't understand

Little Kenny Knottingburg: How Old Are You?

Little Kenny Knottingburg, how old are you?
I'm just one, but I'm going on two

Little Kenny Knottingburg, what will you do at the age of three?
Go into the forest and mess with honeybees

Little Kenny Knottingburg, where will you be at the age of four?
Down on the corner, begging from the poor

Little Kenny Knottingburg, what will you do at the age of five?
I'll just be getting over the experience of the honeybee hives

Little Kenny Knottingburg, I want to know about the age of six
I'll be getting my first job laying high rise building bricks

Little Kenny Knottingburg, what will you do at the age of seven?
I'll begin doing my best to get a free ticket to heaven

Little Kenny Knottingburg, you're getting close to the age of eight
Yeah, I know … and I'm looking for a mate

Little Kenny Knottingburg, have you thought about the age of nine?
I'm going to get married just as soon as I have time

Little Kenny Knottingburg, you've done a lot in life, but what about the age of ten?
Once I finish doing everything, I think I'll start all over again

Little Kenny Knottingburg, your name is sort of strange
My mother only gave it to me so that it would be easier for me to change

Looking Within to Decide

Some thoughts mean more because they bring the inner person out
As they express deep feelings for those they care about

There are good days in life and others that are better still
They can all be worthless without expressing how you really feel

Honest thoughts matter much when expressed as intended
It helps to talk and communicate without attempting to offend

There are women and men who cherish the ground their loved ones tread
There are men and women who are grateful for the partners they wed

There are painful things in life that we accept as we are bound to do
We wouldn't change some things we experience that have helped us get through

I have often heard others say, "Beauty is skin deep"
Perhaps when looking beyond the beauty seen, they will find the truth they seek

Tall, dark, and handsome is what we often choose to see when looking at a man
Are these qualities worthy of a lifetime commitment if he cheats again and again?

Women prepare themselves with pretty clothes, makeup, hair, and some doubt
Beauty and acceptance seem to negate their intelligence as they ignore the shout

… to avoid the presenting encounter because that person is not the one for you
It helps to listen to ourselves deep within and to lingering thoughts, as a rule

Respect of self and adherence to principle to avoid being used or feeling like a fool
Don't be discouraged, keep your head high, and use wisdom as your best tool

It isn't hair, makeup, good looks, or clothes that make you the best partner at hand
Look within to decide if your heart's along for the ride with this woman or man

Why Doesn't Somebody Give?

Why is it so hard to want to see others live?
Why do we sometimes refuse to support their lives and give?

Is there a reason for the hunger that they share?
Many live a life of wealth, while others live one of despair

Have you looked them over... their lives day by day?
Have you ever heard a hungry child have very much to say?

Have you ever even seen their breakfast ... it is not a very hearty meal
If you think about a few of these things then maybe you will give

Why doesn't somebody give to save the lives of their fellow man?
I have little, and yet I choose to give what little I can

Money isn't the only means in life to give of one's self in deed
Consider your available time in life an opportunity to help those in need

Thanks in advance!

My Nobility at Risk

I am no longer a baby or a young girl, small in height
Neither am I the fair maiden awaiting my shining knight

I've traveled from village to village and from town to town
I feel like I'm running out of time as the maids extend my gowns

I seldom eat and I walk and ride daily, but my waist continues to expand
As a member of the nobility, I finally accept that I need to find that man

We were together for one night alone and that was all it took
I can't inform my parents of the knight I slept with after only one look

My noble family has a reputation and they would be in ruins and shattered
They want a grandchild and will permit me to choose who I deem matters

I believe my knight to be noble and willing to marry me soon
I have to trust in my faith in him or my child and I are doomed

I have but to tell him of the results of our brief interlude in the carriage
For him to petition for a license and ask for my hand in marriage

The trip was over and I found his lovely home with relief
I entered the foyer and met his lady wife and six beautiful babes in brief

My Wish, Dream, and Prayer

I wish some day for the better that this world would change
I dream that people smile more without seeing it as strange

I hope more people will rejoice and praise God as they sing
I want memories to be long as we recollect the happiness he brings

My prayer is simple as I think of the human race
Treat each other with love, kindness, respect, and grace

My wish is that from the time we are on this great earth
We never forget the connection experienced with the giving of birth

In my dreams the strength of pulling together is not hard to do
When we are divided is when we struggle to get through

I pray we triumph as we take a chance with one another
My hope is to accept through blood and heart that we are sisters and brothers

My wish, dream, and prayer is for the race separation to fall apart
I want people to feel the beauty inherent in togetherness and a fresh start

You ... Yourself!

Leaving behind your heart in grief
What you're thinking of causes a great relief

As you forget the feelings of the others you've harmed
You go forward trying not to look back in pained alarm

No one is perfect, as in life you learn later on
You learn that you don't really miss something until it's gone

You were told that it's never too late to turn back
It becomes a saying to base your mistakes upon when it's experience you lack

You discover things in life that are worth your time on their behalf
They allow you to step away from being serious and, on the rare occasion, laugh

It's up to you ... yourself ... to acknowledge and let go of the rueful past
It is up to you to have strength of mind in the future once the die is cast

It's Strange

It's strange how life forms all on its own
How it makes things look easier as we travel to and from

It's strange this determination we have to succeed from within
The way we moan with a loss and rejoice when we win

It's strange when we believe there's no way out because no one has the will to go
It's strange to fear the obvious and stranger to be fearful of what we do not know

It seems strange to seek the easy terms of a serious debate
It's like arguing without making a point until the time grows late

It's strange how we agree that it's not too late to start a debate all over again
… insisting that tomorrow will enlighten everyone enough to fully understand

It's strange how we finally learn that not everyone in the world is cruel
It strange how it becomes a personal choice to be flexible or stubborn as a mule

The prejudice, the poverty, the names that we are all called
It's strange how they were formed by us as we built the color barrier walls

It's strange how there's no one answer to all of our prayers
Life sure would be beautiful if everyone could just treat each other fair!

Out in the Country

Out in the country, on a slowly winding road leading to a small shack
There wasn't much to look at while following the dirt tracks

In this old shack lived an old couple who were content and well kept
They often smiled as they talked about how they were no longer in debt

The man was shy and low in spirit to all but his homely little wife
This shy little man always seemed to know the true meaning of life

Out in the country now the little couple moved on, taking with them their good souls
Their small shack fell to the ground the day they died leaving behind a small sink hole

Sonny and the Yankee

Sonny was American and the Yankee was not
When Sonny met the Yankee he told her how he got shot

The Yankee was a lady and had the ways of a man
She was quick on her feet and faster with her hands

When Sonny returned to the states to meet his loving gal
He found his Yankee in the arms of his oldest pal

Sonny went in and saw his Yankee's beautiful face
He knew the war wasn't over and he intended to plead his case

Sonny nodded at his buddy and told the Yankee he was still in love with his girl
As he turned to walk away, she yelled, "Sonny, you're my whole world"

They've been married for fifty years and have six children that are strong
Sonny and his Yankee knew that with their love nothing would ever go wrong

How Can I Help You ... Lost in Between

It is a game he plays in more ways than one
For me it is work and for him it is fun

Your socks are worn your feet are bare
I want to help to show I care

You are agitated ... your mind is away
Your temper is short ... not in a mood to play

I want to help to show I care
I'll always be close should you need me there

My heart drops as you frown
I look away as disappointment abounds

Friends and lovers you must please
I am left with but a small portion of your ease

How can I help you, I often say ... for my love is strong
The hurt I feel perhaps is wrong

My words to you I mean no harm
Your gestures say you are alarmed

I review my comments and see no ill intent
Dare I speak again, when you twist what I meant?

Your work is plenty and your task list a full load
How can I help you ... as the full extent unfolds

It is simple what I feel with these five words from the heart
I search within as I watch you struggle and begin to fall apart

I want to help and send forth a silent plea
Will my words and the presence be enough or will you ask me to leave?

Happy Valentine's Day, My Love

You are the sunshine in my life, the joy in my heart
Without your love and understanding, I will surely fall apart

My love for you has blossomed with each passing year
My love for you grows stronger as it always will, my dear

Happy Valentine's Day my love, and yes I love you so
May our hearts together be always entwined as throughout life we go

Happy Valentine's Day, My Love!

Morie

There was a time when I would allow nothing to interfere with my love for you
Frankie, you were my heart, my love, my desires come true

Our marriage, the vows spoken in song …
mean little to me now that you've gone

I cry, I pray, as I sort through what was done
and then I realize that life for me has only just begun

Your absence has allowed me to grow strong
It outlasted your painful reminders to me when the weight was on

The pain has numbed and I no longer feel as though I am alone
Instead I chose to establish goals to correct your wrongs

Sure, I was sad, but I changed my pace
by removing the hurt and putting joy in its place

Do You Love Me?

Do you love me, or do you not?
You told me once but I forgot

I do believe that God above
Created you for me to love

He picked you out from all the rest
Because he knew I could love you the best

I had a heart and it was true
But now it is gone from me to you

Take this heart as I have done
You'll have two and I'll have none

When I get to heaven I'll wait for you there
I'll look for you often as I watch from the golden stairs

If you're not there by Judgment Day
I'll know you went the other way

I'll give the Angels back their wings
... Golden hearts and other things

And just to prove my love is true
... I'll go to hell just for you

If I Had Two Days to Live, I Would ...

If I had two days to live, I'd write poetry to no end on the first day
Then live a little in my own way

Life is short and I'd learn to enjoy it
I'd encourage someone to do something to show their wit

I'd lie in a field and look up at the sky
I'd watch the people as they walked by

Once I realized there would soon be no more time
on the last day I'd explore the wonders of my mind

If I had only two days to live
I would offer myself to help others and freely give

With only two days to live, I would seek to understand
Why life's so short and why you never get to experience it again

When I got on my knees and began to pray
I wasn't sure of what I'd say

I'd ask God to forgive all of the wrong
of the people still here and of those that are gone

And when my two days had come to an end
I would say thank you to all of my supportive friends

1980

Fraternal Twins

There were preventative measures taken so that pregnancy didn't occur
And yet the ultrasound showed that there you were

Intrauterine device (IUD) gently pressing in on your forehead
Grateful to God that it wasn't embedded instead

Big brown eyes you cannot miss
Strength revealed as you raise your small fist

Tight curly hair placed on your perfectly round head
A cute little mouth smacking for food to be fed

Long brown legs kicking up a storm
Seeking the attention for which you were born

Cute button nose scrunched up as you yell
Crying your heart out for a very short spell

All of a sudden you make contact with a small bundle lying close
Your little hand appearing as you reach for the one you trust the most

Your tiny twin appearing to sleep through your frustrating storm
Unaware of changes to 9 months of shared space before you two were born

Although your brother is smaller and doesn't fidget as much
He does seem to respond to your sweet gentle touch

He was 4 pounds and 2 ounces to your 6 pounds 11
The two of you are blessings God sent to us from heaven

Missing You

While you're away and I am unable to see your face
I'm sad and I cry as I look at your picture in your place

There is no fun with you gone
There is no one to talk to while I'm alone

You made the sun, you made the moon
How I pray we'll be together again soon

There are no walks in the park for you and I
And when I'm alone, I recall our goodbye

No, not goodbye, but "until we are together again"
you see, my love for you is forever, my husband

Sure, I'm lonely and yes, I'm sad
but my thoughts of you are more beautiful than any I have ever had

As long as the sun has a shine and the sky is blue
Darling I'll always be loving and missing you

With You Gone

The sun won't shine as brightly as before
My eyes don't glow so brightly anymore

Our evenings in the park will my remembrance be
but they are to be cherished as you are to me

The laughs, the joy of having you near
Will be gone with you no longer here

I'll pray, I'll wait, and I'll occupy my time
… as I think of the beauty that you leave behind

Instead of sunshine, there will always be rain
… because with you gone, life won't be the same

On the inside, I know I am sad
On the outside, I'll smile as I think of the good times we've had

It would be wrong to lie and say I won't cry
for with the love I feel for you, I didn't ever want to say goodbye

With my dreams and fantasies, I'll attempt to enlighten the day
I accept that I am going to miss you until your return, in every single way

I'll look at your picture, remembering your walk, talk, and loving smile
It is then that you'll be close to me … at least for a little while

I Love You, and I know it will always last
Though when I think of you in the future, it will be full of loving memories from our past

Miss Fat Pat

Pat was sort of fat, but she was not a wobbly cat
She moved slowly and was heavy if in your lap was where she sat

She was mean at times, but mostly she was very sweet
Her family finally realized that her only problem was she loved to eat

She went on a diet but couldn't resist food
It seems she was always in a very hungry mood

Poor Pat was ruining her life because she was too stout
Until her family read a book that really made things work out

Pat wanted to run with the other cats and be active in play
With a change to her diet and activity, Pat began to lose her excess weight

The Democracy of Today

The democracy of today is not one filled with expected equality
The people seem to be lacking in voice during the final legalities

The value of a democracy is for everyone to have their say
People are inspired in this free country to expect to work for fair pay

Exploring the varying aspects of the democracy of today as it exists
Can only strengthen our resolve to eliminate any segregation lists

If we treat each other with respect and regard, knowledge remains on track
As the democracy of today prepares for the future, history will have the facts

We learn to honor the meaning of democracy as we create lasting changes
Democracy ensures choice and voice for all people regardless of their language

Did You Know...?

Did you know that the sun refuses to shine
That my love for you will last throughout the end of time

That the moon has a fake glow
That true love will always show

That the stars are all in a huddle
That falling in love leaves many puddles

That the snow melts away slowly, as does my heart
That the sleet falls hard as did I from the start

That love not sought could prove worthwhile
That no matter how far apart, we seldom saw the miles

That I dream of the precious day
... when I can see again my sweetheart's face

That when you return you may choose not to be mine?
I'll not forget my promise to love you throughout the end of time

Decisions

Leaving the military is a tough decision and a difficult choice
If I am to live with my decision, I must listen primarily to my voice

This is the beginning and I plan to forge ahead
I've looked forward to this day with joy, fear, and dread

I won't allow the negative opinions of others to deter my frame of mind
I plan to do my very best to stand out and shine

Decisions are not always easy to make
There's always something to consider and there can be much at stake

As a parent with a responsibility to small children in your care
It's you they depend upon and you that need to be there

Employment is a must …
Because they look to you with open hearts of trust

Assigning someone else to their care in order that I meet an obligation
Was not a decision I chose to make, although there was much contemplation

I chose them above the career of my choice, finding it worth the sacrifice
I placed my future in the hands of God, depending on his guidance and advice

There is no turning back or placing guilt on anyone else
I made the right decision and am pleased with myself

1982

The Battle of Regret

There are many wars fought between the faces of this earth
Today's fighting is just as bad as the others, which were started first

People are not as they once were when they fought for freedom and liberty
It is as though we no longer have a say in a country that believes in democracy

The battle of regret is one that has yet to be forgotten
The seeds that were sown years ago are still providing stink to the rotten

I believe that the battle of regret is fought one on one from within
We can each choose to do what's right or we can choose to give in

The Death of A Poem

A poem is often livened up by its creative words and rhyme
The death of a poem is a loss to the reader's interest of mind

"Live it up" is the motto of a few poem writer's quest
The death of a poem may put the author to a test

A poem by a master poet brings out an emotion as the readers are caught
It keeps the readers wanting more as they engage in thought

The death of a poem is not an option because no poem wants to die
If the poets fall into a slump, they won't give up without another try

I love writing poetry and the way poems make me think
My hope is that readers feel the emotions entailed in each creative link

A Lack of Faith

I have played many games, but basketball beats them all
Because you can't be too short and you can't be too tall

When you lose a game, you have to hold back your tears
There are times when you score points and everyone cheers

There was a girl on our team who was about to give up one day
We gathered around her on the bench, encouraging her to play

She picked up the ball ...
as she heard the coach call

She went to the floor with pride in every step
making every goal without very much help

Her lack of faith didn't keep her sad and low
Later, she said her team helped her to battle and win against her greatest foe

A lack of faith can keep you from winning many of life's games
Believe in yourself--you're not alone, and a call for help isn't always in vain

Let This Day Be a Special Day

I'm up early and coming down the stairs
I grab my toe as I bump into a dining room chair

I stop to think about my day as I see a ray of sunshine
I smile as I prepare breakfast and sit down to dine

I hum as I work into the middle of the day
When I'm done, I look up and begin to pray

"Oh God let this day be a special day ...
Help me to complete my tasks and not get in anyone's way"

I prepare dinner for my family, making it a hearty meal
I write a letter to my friend as I ask God to help her heal

This day that was here is now gone as night returns
I've forgotten my troubles as I realize I have time to burn

Before I know it, I'm ready for bed because it's so late
As I fall asleep, I dream until the morning when I wake

Traveling Home

I've traveled high and I've traveled low
Trying to get home to a father I don't know

I know I have to travel until I find my way
Even if I travel all night and all day

I've packed my bags and I'm ready to go
On my way to Heaven to a father I don't know

If you want to come and join in my journey home
Pack your bags and we will travel along

1983

Lost Art

Art is a part of our daily lives, it is what we choose to reveal
Art is what we make of it, of how we display what we feel

Art comes from within and it is who we are
It can set you back or it can take you far

Art is what we dream
It may not be what it seems

The enjoyment of art is to each his own
To appreciate art, one need not stand alone

One man's Michelangelo
May be another man's Picasso

Art is to be seen, enjoyed, admired, and constructively criticized
The viewer may have emotions of love, hate, or pride

Art is a musician tuning his instrument before he plays
Art is a ballerina dancing before an audience on stage

Art is not just on a canvas or a creation from a sculptor's mind
Art is what we make of it and can remain so throughout time

Don't Look at Me

Don't look at me, once I was beautiful and so proud
Now I am all weathered and they want to throw me out

Don't look at me, once I stood strong and grand for all to see
Even Presidents and Generals were in awe of me

Don't look at me, I'm ugly and unappealing to the eye
Don't look at me, it is because of you that I must die

Look at me, and weep in deep sorrow
Look at me today because I'll not be here tomorrow

Look at me and remember what it was like to walk my halls each day
Look at me and pay homage to my rot and decay

Look at me and think of what I stood for so long ago
Look at me and shamefully hang your heads low

Look at me, this once great building that held history of present and past
Look at me, once you stopped caring I can no longer last

Look at me, the museum that once held artifacts of present and past
Look at me, once you stopped caring I can no longer last

Look at the great "White Hall", once the military's pride
Don't look at me, I no longer represent as I disintegrate from the inside

My Symptoms of Pain

I have a pain at the back of my head and behind my left ear
It hurts so badly until it brings me to tears

It causes pressure at the side of my neck as it gravitates down my back
Sometimes it's difficult to walk as I am surprised by the sudden attack

The pain is so strong until my neck feels strained
It's getting so bad until it feels like it's hurting my brain

My eyes sometimes refuse to open unless it's dark
My symptoms of pain can be lasting with a reality that's stark

When the pain is intense, I feel as though I'm going insane
I often find it difficult to live with my symptoms of pain

I am lucky that it only bothers me off and on
And that this is the first time it has lasted this long

After a few days the pain has decreased in intensity, I surmise
It returns with a vengeance, leaving me to once again close my eyes

1984

I Have Found What I Was After

I had a precious token of little cost
It was a shiny silver dollar that I long ago lost

It was old and worn with the surface nearly flat
I often rubbed the edges before I went up to bat

I guess you could say it was my lucky charm
I'm always looking for it when I visit the family farm

I remember the last time I flipped it, the sun was shining bright
I never saw where it landed and I looked for it far into the night

Many years have passed; the farm is up for sale and I have the deed
I looked over the property as I contemplated beneath my favorite tree

As my fingers touched the ground, I brushed aside the dirt, nice and slow
I've found what I was after: my silver dollar without its precious glow

Easter FUN

Easter is a time of year where we have lots of fun
We look for eggs together as we laugh and run

It takes a lot of enjoyment and togetherness to enjoy the hunt
We search everywhere, behind trees, rocks, old cars, and junk

I enjoy the Easter holiday and my new clothes are fine
People seem to come together and have a really good time

Easter day makes me smile because I always know what to do
… find the eggs and gobble them up as fast as I can chew

YUM!

1987

You Remind Me of ...

You remind me of my life assorted in the ghetto down south
I was always going places and running my big mouth

I know you aren't from the ghetto, but it's almost the same
You live in a lovely house but you are known for your dirty name

You remind me of a dream I had not so long ago
Of how someday the world would change, gradually and slow

I've never given up that dream so strange
Because someday I believe this world will positively change

You remind me of who I'll choose not to be
You remind me I need to hold onto all of my possibilities

Look at the People

Look at the people and wonder what's on their minds
Do you think they have easy lives, or are they on hard times?

Some of them work in the fields of satisfaction, love, and joy
Some of them have few clothes and food for their little girls and boys

You may sacrifice your one and only hope of grace
You look at the people and find yourself unable to cope with them face-to-face

You are reminded of your childhood, the way you've lived and grown
It also reminds you of life challenges now that you're on your own

As you look at the people, you decide it is not too late to pick up on hope
You've finally looked at the people face-to-face and realized what you have to do to cope

You look at the people and realize you are not alone
You look at the people and accept that at last you are home

Spiritual Food Cake

You start with 1 cup of thoughts followed by 1 cup of consideration for each other
Add 2 cups of sacrifice followed quickly by 3 cups of well beaten faults and a fist of love

Pour in 4 cups of forgiveness and mix it up really good
Add a few tears of joy as you voice how much you understood

Toss in a pinch of sympathy and a smidgen of sorrow
Then flavor the mixture with little gifts of love and kindness borrowed

Pour in 4 cups of prayer and a whole lot of faith
That's just to lighten the weight of the ingredients and improve the taste

Test the texture for success of great heights in character and Christian living
After pouring it all into your daily life, prepare yourself for the giving

Bake over the hours at 350 degrees with humor, kindness, and warmth without cold
Serve with a smile any time, and it will satisfy the hunger of starved souls

Store unused or excess supplies in your heart pantry for future spiritual cakes
Welcome presenting opportunities to enfold and share with all willing to partake

Spiritual food cake is a recipe full of lasting love which is often sought
It's a form of nourishment freely given with ingredients that can't be bought

1989

Graduation

We finally reached that day
And I get to say … "I Thank You"

It wasn't always fair
But you three were always there … "I Thank You"

Graduation is here and the schedules have been rough
There were times I wanted to quit when the going got tough

But the three of you encouraged me to go on
As you helped me to care for the children until I was done … "I Thank You"

Carlos, Patti and Faye, all friends of my heart
I'm forever grateful for your support in my life from the start … "I Thank You"

The graduation confirms my effort with the final degree
My precious four children and you are so meaningful to me … "I Thank You"

1990

The Flower of My Dreams

The rose is the flower of my dreams among flowers
It stands out in the garden during a pouring rain shower

The rose blooms are of a variety in colors so bright
Their beauty so memorable as they grow in height

I smile at the pinks, reds, yellows, and fashionable multicolor tips
As I wonder about the occasion when the next patron will request a rose clip

For some, the rose represents a chance to celebrate
For others, it is often given as a gift during a date

The flower of my dreams is the rose of perfection with thorns that can harm
The rose is a reminder of the world's reality and how beauty can hurt as it charms

If You Want to Be Truly Happy

If you want to be truly happy, decide on what it means to you
If you want to be truly happy, seek contentment in the things you do

If you want to be truly happy, find a smile and prolong its stay
If you want to be truly happy, ask God to help show you the way

If you want to be truly happy, search deep down inside
If you want to be truly happy, consider life's nuances you choose to abide

If you want to be truly happy, stand still and stop running away
If you want to be truly happy, face your fears and demons each day

If you want to be truly happy, never allow others to decide your fate
If you want to be truly happy, live your life … it's never too late

If you want to be truly happy, the decision is yours to make
If you want to be truly happy, love yourself with as much love as you can take

1992

Silly Sandy

Sandy was a funny girl and she made the class laugh all the time
The teacher thought Sandy was funny and didn't seem to mind

Her friends thought she was funny because she made them smile
Her mom thought she was silly but also a funny child

Sandy told jokes to everyone, which made her feel good
Everybody laughed at her silly jokes, which she told because she could

One day her mom got sick and Sandy told a funny joke as she set with her
Sandy's mom laughed at the joke saying she felt a lot better

Silly Sandy kept telling jokes enjoying the happiness they'd bring
The smiles and laughter of others made her little heart sing

Transition

Until the time comes when we can get ahead
There are times when we have to take what we can get instead

Not everyone will get a job of their dreams
Some will have to settle for less, it seems

That is not to say you should give up without a fight
Use your willpower to survive the struggles of life

With any transitions, there are concerns and fear
It is the determination to survive which propels you into gear

There will be offers made and promises set in stone
There are many who will excel through perseverance alone

You are an individual whose life has perhaps just begun
Will you meet the challenges, or will you turn and run?

1995

I Feel So Dead Inside....

I feel so dead inside, afraid and all alone
I hate myself, but when I was with you, those feelings were all gone

You told me you wanted me--you said you were sure
I gave you my heart and took hold of a love most pure

My soul bit hard, my heart wanted more
So I closed my eyes and opened the door...

That was stupid, I made a mistake
The last part of my shattered heart you did break

I trusted your words, I believed your eyes
God blessed your kiss, but your lips told lies, love was life but life dies

I feel so dead inside, you threw me away
I begged you to take me back, I wanted to stay

It's easy to stop ... easier to quit ...
To take my love and treat me like s...!

That's what you did ... that's what was done
Now I'm alone and without anyone

I hope you live long, I hope you live well
Don't die like me ... love's death is hell

(I Feel So Dead Inside....)

I feel so dead inside ... afraid and all alone
I want you back so bad, but that story's done

Life now gone ... love now lost ...
I'm colder than ice ... my new heart blackened by frost

I used to love ... I used to know how ...
But now that's all gone ... I've ripped it all out

I can't hurt ... although I'm all alone
The feeling is lost ... the Demon has won

I miss love ... true, unknown, eternal love
I feel so dead inside

You and Me

Do you remember the day we first met?
How we laughed with joy as under the large pine tree we sat

Have you forgotten the words you so sweetly spoke to me?
The ones that brought so many tender memories

Have you forgotten how you held me so tenderly?
As you whispered words of endearment to me

Have you forgotten how we asked our parents for our marriage consent?
How we jumped for joy as to the justice of the peace we went

Have you forgotten about our first child born?
How beautiful his touch as together we dressed him in his first clothes to be worn

… And do you remember or think about the things we say today?
How we constantly complain of everything we each do and say

Have we lost our love, you and me?
… The one which together we held so tenderly

A Mother's Suffering ... Don't Give Up

When you're feeling down and out
And no one in the world knows what you're about ... don't give up

Remember the good times together you have had
Think of the joys provided when you were sad ... don't give up

The memories from our mothers that we will always hold dear
It's okay to let go and to cry the occasional river of tears ... don't give up

You're busy holding everyone together until you don't realize you're falling apart
No burden can you bear alone, sharing the load is a start ... don't give up

You budget the household finances, making sure there's plenty to eat
When was the last time you simply relaxed and soaked your feet ... don't give up

You worry about the welfare and life of each family member in disarray
You need to let go ... relax, have fun, and find time to play ... don't give up

You try to do it all and wonder why you feel in despair
Look within yourself for comfort and to others who genuinely care ... don't give up

Seldom do you smile and it's more precious than gold
You reflect on your faults, frown and depress your very soul ... don't give up

There's meaning to life with its many joys, ups and downs
There's no need to sacrifice yourself to achieve goals you've already found ...
don't give up

I Carry My Cross ... Memories

You made me stand up and carry my cross
You made me stronger and I accepted my loss

When Momma died and they took her body away
I bore the pain, though I didn't want to stay

I hurt so badly when I knew she was gone
I wanted my momma ... I felt so all alone

You made me stand up and bear my cross
You made me stronger and I accepted my loss

Then my daddy was gone and his body taken away
Dear God, I hurt so bad ... I didn't want to stay

You made me stand up and carry my cross
You made me stronger and I accepted my loss

Within me, I walked through the ashes where his body had burned
I sat down and cried and prayed he'd return

You made me stand up and carry my cross
You made me stronger and I accepted my loss

My brother was kind and good to all
When hit by a drunk driver, he heeded your call

I became angry and frustrated and I didn't understand
So much pain and so many demands

You made me stand up and carry my cross
You made me stronger and I accepted my loss

Friendship

Kindness is precious, true friendships rare
I thank you for both and your willingness to share

No one said the road to contentment would be straight, narrow, or refined
The many curves of life are shared while traveling the roads of life one day at a time

Our choices are an aspect of the decisions made as we continue to abide
Our wisdom reiterates ongoing success through life's many roller coaster rides

Wherever you go, whatever dreams you fulfill
Remember to slow down and separate fantasy from real

Hold on to the good times while learning from the bad in passing
Don't forget the heartfelt friendship that is everlasting

About the Author

Writing began as a form of escape for me from the world of reality, allowing for self-expression while I lived in a foster home with my siblings and many other children. Some of the poems were written without thought, while others were written as a form of communication without the element of verbal interaction. The poems weren't always about anything or anyone specific.

I grew up learning and believing that children weren't always meant to be seen or heard, so I learned to be creative in my invisibility while hiding in plain sight. My poetry allowed me an "out" in order to somehow feel connected to something during frequent periods of aloneness.

I have lived in Alaska with my beautiful family for over 27 years. I have a husband of over 40 years and together we have, among our extended family, six beautiful adult children and six grandchildren.

$22.95
ISBN 978-0-9981443-1-3

www.ingramcontent.com/pod-product-compliance
Lightning Source LLC
Chambersburg PA
CBHW041524220426
43670CB00002B/26